Confessions of

a

Porn Addict

Crow Hollow Books

Confessions of a Porn Addict

poems by Jay Sizemore

Published by Crow Hollow Books
Nashville, TN 37075

Copyright © 2015, Jay Sizemore

Manufactured print on demand

10 9 8 7 6 5 4 3 2 1

ISBN 978-0692494134

Cover art creative attribution to Martin de Pasquale.
www.martindepasquale.com
Used with permission of the artist.

I wrote this for myself. I could dedicate it to an ex who hated my habits, but that would just be cruel, though maybe not as cruel as her jealousy of Jenna Jameson.

TABLE OF CONTENTS

Job interview

Tell us a little about yourself.
The walls of my childhood
were thin, made of metal and wood paneling,
and I taped my posters up, because tacks
would not go through. My mother taught me
to shut my eyes during the dirty parts,
pink melding into the light between my fingers,
so now I'm a pornography addict.
Nervousness seems to build bombs in my neck,
I have Tourette's without the curse words,
and I pick psoriatic scabs off my scalp
like a gorilla obsessed with decomposition.
Some nights I can't sleep
because I don't trust the silence.

What is your greatest weakness?
I hate lying, but I lie to myself.
I say I don't care, but I examine every twitch
of the eyes in my direction, scrutinize
every pucker of wrinkled skin in their faces,
assess the gestures of meaningless movements
like a tree trying to siphon water from the wind.

Why do you want to work for us?
Alone with my thoughts, I would eat myself.

My perversion

Barely concealed, each woman
waits for my eyes to betray me,
a self conscious stab of silence,
pulling at shirts for more fabric.

Don't look. Stare at their throats,
lock eyes until it's uncomfortable,
steal glances from fish-mouthed faces
being reeled up to breathlessness.

Tiny wrists, collar bones,
the meaty base of a palm,
the way fingers hug cigarettes
and curl like leaves.

Everything is sexual,
a raw nerve worn like a halo,
denying the tension drawn
between spoken words like caramel.

It's all imaginary; these bodies
trap all this light wanting to escape,
long legs, hips, the smooth valley
of a lower back, just energy changing forms,

all of us lightning rods
chasing the sound of thunder.

Love walks into a bar and says

this is all for me, a cathedral of mistakes.
She lies on the floor and spreads her legs,
making a snow angel in the grime,
sticky beer and cigarette butts.
She invites men to pour their drinks
into her second mouth,
but they just stare,
aroused, and ashamed of their arousal.
She says, "fuck me, this is the voice of consent,
this is the voice of my power over you,"
and no one moves, someone whispers,
"this makes me uncomfortable,"
shuffles his feet, kicking a bottle.
"Aren't you afraid of dying alone?"
she strokes a hand up her slit
and a swath of spiders issues from the hole,
scattering in all directions,
they evaporate into wisps of fog,
leaving a scent of sweet candied perfume.
The men shriek like children,
cowering against every wall,
throwing themselves over the bar
as she laughs the way wasps must laugh,
a high-pitched buzz like paper-thin wings.
And suddenly she's gone,
like a cherry fire scraped under a boot,
leaving only a dark mark on the dingy ground.
The music picks back up, and the clinking ambience
of alcohol dreams resumes, each sip shaking
the shock off the crash. It's not long
and one man says to another,
"When you going to fuck that girl?"

Narcissism born

The clitoris is the only god
worthy of being worshipped,
but we've been made ashamed
of our love for sex,
the pornography pews
are best sat in alone,
hidden from the stained glass
and the snow globes
where we keep our truths.

My selfishness is a genetic flaw,
passed down from an absent father
who's never let me run out
of analogies for ghosts,
when new ghosts are born every second
and old ones haunt my veins
like names never given to children.

Selfishness and loneliness
are stripes on the same animal,
something without wings
that is convinced it once knew how to fly,
but forgot how in mid-dive,
falling into the open mouth
of a lust that feels
too obscene to touch.

Free Porn

She smiles at you
through the HD screen,
a hot and horny
sex-crazed teen,
wanting only the
only wanting
to double-click
and double-click,
to touch her lips
with another man's dick,
to stroke her skin
with another man's hands,
feeling her warmth
and slickness of sweat
as real as it gets, the triple X pixels
of an obscene wet dream,
to pull her hair
and make her scream,
slap her ass
and lick that tramp stamp
with someone else's tongue,
maybe let someone else
join in on the fun,
she wants you to,
she wants *you* too,
her eyes say she is ready
to suck, fuck, and swallow
every dollar and every cent
through your cock
like a straw,
as if you ejaculate
quarters, nickels, and dimes,
and her pussy, her asshole,
her mouth are nothing more

than digital piggy bank slots,
so satisfy your lust,
and fill her up,
give her exactly
what you know she wants,
just don't cut yourself
on all the broken glass.

Adult Film Actress

She's a sultry swan, with paper feathers,
torn from the pages of bibles.
The small of her back is a river bed

stony and smooth as credit fraud.
She's a souvenir bottle opener,
her lips mated apostrophes,

putting her words in quotes,
her blowjobs in guillotines.
She's a flotation device.

A Lesson Learned

Mother, I'm sorry,
I saw you naked,
through the crack in the door,
you never noticed me,
your head was down,
your hands outstretched and tangled
in the matted thicket of his chest.
The morning light diffused through
the white pull-down blinds
lit up the room like some kind
of cheap porno fantasy,
if I was old enough to have fantasies,
which I was not,
and the monster never flinched,
stretched out on the plain white sheets,
his hands locked behind his head,
his eyes closed,
and your lips on his penis,
stroking backward from the black swath
of his pubic hair,
as I gently pulled the door shut
and ran back to my bed,
without making a sound,
my face red, my thoughts confused,
learning the valuable lesson
of knocking.

Admissions

I count the steps I take every morning to my car,
yesterday it was 96, today 108,
filling my head with the white noise of numbers
perhaps to block out the monotony and the numbness
of a routine that dwells like a year inside of a blink.

My internal voice is like road rage from the seventies,
sometimes calling people niggers just because
it wants to hate something other than the cave it echoes
inside,
even if that hate isn't real, has never consumed me
like the guilt of knowing I do not love enough.

I feel like a drunk on a tightrope,
wobbling back and forth over that brink
as if pulled by opposing moons
formed from broken landscapes of my heart,
the place where all dreams start and die.

I'm a pornography thief, an addict to the idea
of getting everything I want, and I will objectify you,
I will think about fucking you while you play
with your cell phone. I worry about being consumed
like a diary soaked in gasoline,
when all these thoughts are phosphorous-tipped.

Ken and Barbie

Her nudity isn't obscene
as long as her hands
cover her nipples,
and everyone pretends
that she doesn't have a vagina
or an asshole down there.

His penis doesn't exist,
a plastic castration
of smooth flesh tones,
a smile on every face
filled with white paint.
His hair doesn't move.

Sex.
No pimples.
Sex.
No cavities.
Sex.
No farting.
Sex.
No fatties.
Sex.
No education.

Habits

She smokes the cigarette
like a dirty habit,
holds the ashtray
away from me
on the bed,
blows the smoke
out the left corner
of her mouth
like a factory whistle
in some fifties cartoon,
but we both know
her real dirty habit
is me.

Covered in sweat
we talk about tattoos,
she has one on her hip
that she says
means she was born
in the wrong generation,
maybe she feels
like an acid flash back
still trapped
in the spinal fluid
of Sir Paul McCartney.

I don't smoke,
but I take her
into my lungs and exhale
a memory of Marlboro-
flavored kisses,
leaving the filter
on the mattress
to watch me

put my clothes on,
letting my regret
scatter like ashes
blown in the gusts
of a summer storm.

When the condom breaks

There's no time to worry
about the possible repercussions
of premarital penetrations,
the sudden warmth involved
with bodily fluid exchanges,
or the cost of prenatal vitamins,

the mind is in another place,
erogenous and animalistic,
oblivious to everything except
the lubrication of sweat and vowels
and the scent of sex
mingled with perfumes,

best to just swap out
the equipment and finish the job
while the intensity
inside the hearts of flesh
still aches and throbs
for the finale
of guttural
moans.

After,
in the quiet,
it's never mentioned,
we lay without clothes
while she collects thoughts
inside tendrils of smoke
and I wait
for the urge
to fuck her again.

Better Decisions

These walls are painted with regret,
and broken promises
linger like ghosts in the halls.

I should have made better decisions.

I took down the bricks
one by one,
only to stack them around myself,
and fill the cracks
with the mortar of words
and whispers in the dark.

I should have made better decisions.

I stood on the banks
of a river without a name
and crossed its waters
only to find
that I liked the view better
from the other side.

I should have made better decisions.

I said goodbye
to the couch and the chair,
and put my clothes
in a much smaller closet,
while you arranged furniture
inside the shoebox
of a gay man.

I should have made better decisions.

I let a stranger in
and gave him the key
that you removed
from your very heart
or a keychain
of that exact same shape.

My new bed

Tonight I sleep in an ashtray,
last night I slept on the couch,
my body squeezed into a space
it was not meant to fit,
like an accordion stuffed into
a coffee can
or a human being inside
a dog house inside a grave
being shoveled over
with eggshells.

I prefer the ashtray,
my feet do not hang
off the edge of my new bed.
Instead, I sleep sound,
I drink in the night whispers
of ghostly conceptions,
the dark stains of
premarital virginity,
phantasms of former selves
that wrap around me
like supernatural blankets.

I dream.
I wake up.
I wash off the scent of smoke,
the aftermath
of living inside
a burning house.

To the girl who kept the replica of my penis

did you ever get it past
those pursed iron lips,
into the succulent juices
your body denied me?

the long con of unrequited lust
couldn't be sated with a tantric blowjob,
your round face bobbing above two small fists
faster and faster until my back arched and twisted
like a suspension bridge in an earthquake.

it was an act of charity
to let you attempt such therapy,
sticking my dick in that foam latex mold
and watching you pour the liquid
into the space it left behind,
still your vagina was a closed mouth,

even after a bottle of vodka
slurred your septic speech,
had you flopping and thrashing
like a fish in a boat,
you couldn't share with me
what others had taken
without permission,
and I don't blame you for that.

A hint of uncertainty

I've lived long enough
but I haven't lived long,
I've seen supermarkets come and go,
wars begin and end, I've watched
small businesses start, then flounder
like puppies drowning in a flood.

I've lived, I've had a life,
I've cried under misfortune's veil
and relished the warm glow
of things working out in my favor
without a college degree.

I've stood at the bedside of someone I love
while they struggled for their final breaths,
I've felt the pride of lifting a giggling child
to touch the ceiling, but I've been too afraid
to come inside my wife without protection,
too afraid to relinquish myself to that selfless act,
to see myself growing in someone else's eyes,
to commit to a future so obscured
by the certitude of failure.

I've avoided that car crash, that slip and fall
ending in a broken neck, that undertow
sucking past my feet, dragging bits of broken shells
out into the depths. I've seen storms uproot
trees that once held tire swings my sister and I
would take turns spinning each other in,
turning the world into a dizzying blur
of skies and fields. I've watched lightning
flash in the windows at night, and wondered
if that electricity could spell my name,
could turn my body into a neon sign.

I've lived. I've abandoned dreams out of convenience,
pawned them for that cheap fix, that 42 inch television
and Toyota Camry with the dented back bumper,
I've lived with the taste of beer on my tongue,
the itch of dry skin in my scalp, the longing
that comes from self-medicating a career,
sleeping half these precious days away
like I'm trying to forget something unforgettable.
I've lived, I've lived, I've lived,
please tell me that I have lived.

Innate actions that make up a day

There's the breathing that never stops,
except for those times when he's asleep,
and he awakes, gasping for breath,
trying to fight out of his skin
that's smothering him.
Thirty-three years spent two minutes
at a time, deciding which pair of pants go best
with whatever shirt that no one will notice,
a t-shirt or a button up,
the gray slip-ons or the cowboy boots.
Toothpaste gets smeared on the bristles
of the brush, vibrating like
an electric dildo against his teeth,
freshening his breath for five minutes
before he swallows another cup of snot.
There's the driving to and from,
the music too loud to listen to the car's
whining belts, singing along out of key,
pounding the snare drum and high-hat
of the steering wheel, while avoiding
the eminent collision with a bitch
who couldn't wait five minutes
to text her boyfriend.
He counts the body segments of the wasp,
dried up and caught in an abandoned
spider web, wonders if it will hang
there all winter, like a soundless wind chime
by his door. Tiny circles of repeating habits
intertwine to fill in the gaps of monotony
with alcohol, acrylic paint, and pre-semen,
oiling the gears of the machine
that pushes forward through this tunnel
filled with reflections and just enough darkness
that one might confuse them for stars.

Proletariat

He tries to play piano,
garbage bags duct taped
over his hands, cinched
at the wrists. Tries to sing
with a mouth full of rocks.

He has a savings account
to which he diverts
a river of pornographic
magazine clippings,
the bones of birds,
crude drawings of male genitalia.

His wife pawned her rings,
spread her legs for debt collectors,
paid for an abortion with a blowjob.
She uses a dollar bill
for a book mark.

The house was turning into cardboard
around them, cups in cabinets
filling with rain water
and goldfish, already homeless.

He sold his guitar for a gallon of milk,
sold the gallon of milk for a quart of gas,
the quart of gas for a shot of gin,
anything to dull his wits long enough for sex,
but found his penis amputated
to pay for weight loss pills.

Indivisible

Zero is indivisible.
You can't share nothing
with someone else.
Emptiness is a self-contained
affliction, or an all-encompassing
void. How can nothing weigh
so much, when it exists inside you?

His eyes are zeroes.
His mouth is a zero.
His heart is a zero.
His asshole is a zero.

Put your lips to his eyes.
Put your tongue in his mouth.
Put your ear to his heart.
Put your nothing in his nothing.

Love is a thunderstorm

gathering moisture from the Earth,
conversations of exhaled breaths
between sets of luminous eyes,
a humidity grows that feeds the clouds.

Layer upon layer builds into a turbulent
static charge, an attraction between
the sky and the ground that must be released,
in a flash of white-hot heat, or a first kiss.

The colors change from deepest blue to
the darkest gray, as the weight of bellies
full of rain swells to bury the sun,
and down drafts make the trees sway,

a shivering hum of rustling leaves and wind,
as they seek shelter in each other's arms
and skin, the pregnant heavens explode,
a downpour of sweat, of flood, of thunder

blending into raucous cries of lust,
while the intensity churns, contorted
by a Coriolis effect into cyclonic fury,
an unstoppable force that twists telephone

poles into splinters like chewed toothpicks,
destroying all ties except those to one another,
lying naked and caressed by rain-soaked grass,
as the tempest fades, a soothing drizzle of light.

Disaster Porn

Just an unspeakable tragedy
on slow-motion repeat,
a skyscraper for each pupil
devoured by gray billows of ash,
watching people jump from windows
to escape the heat.
Do you believe in God?
Answer with a bullet in the head,
the sounds of burst rounds
echoing down a high school hall,
black and white CCTV footage
like a silent film recorded in Hell
an unspeakable tragedy.
Watching the edge of the water
suck back like a deep breath,
minutes before the tidal swell
filled 460,000 lungs,
entire villages scrubbed off the land
like old paint from a house.
Such a horrible tragedy.
Over 400 rounds of ammunition,
two handguns, a knife, and a hammer,
time to go home and change clothes
after the first shots were fired.
Barricading the doors,
blocking bodies with bodies
thirty-two lives gone,
an unforeseeable tragedy.
Hillside slums built on an atom bomb,
no infrastructure to prevent mudslides,
300,000 buried in the shifting ground,
debris opening like a mouth
to swallow the sleeping.
Such an unspeakable tragedy.
The capillaries pulsate and irises open,
the heart rate quickens
as breaths grow shallow.
Throats run dry, demand drinks be served.
The channel never changes
from the unspeakable.

September 11th, 2001
September 11th, 2001
September 11th, 2001
September 11th, 2001
September 11th, 2001
September 11th, 2001
April 20th, 1999
April 20th, 1999
April 20th, 1999
April 20th, 1999
April 20th, 1999
April 20th, 1999
April 20th, 1999
December 26th, 2004
December 26th, 2004
December 26th, 2004
December 26th, 2004
December 26th, 2004
December 26th, 2004
December 26th, 2004
April 16th, 2007
April 16th, 2007
April 16th, 2007
April 16th, 2007
April 16th, 2007
April 16th, 2007
April 16th, 2007
April 16th, 2007
January 12th, 2010
January 12th, 2010
January 12th, 2010
January 12th, 2010
January 12th, 2010
January 12th, 2010
today today today
today today today
today today today
today today today
today today today
today today today

a good drunk

It takes a good drunk
to rub the tarnish from the world.
The poison burns away sadness,
veins like rusted power cables
flooded with battery acid,
a corrosive cleansing.
When the burning lurches
its way out of the hole,
into the white porcelain bowl,
the tears run freely, leaving a milky residue.
All you want to do is sleep.

A shuddering vibrancy enters
like light splintered through
sticky lashes, a hangover headache
that detaches the skull from the body
like a deflating helium balloon,
making steps wobbly
as a wind blown shadow.
The edges are hard,
crisp, and new again.
The sun's warmth heals with saturation,
rekindling the richness of existence
that monotony had drained away.

Almost date raped

He never fooled himself into believing
that music could start a revolution,
that words could stop a war
the way darkness could drain
color from a tan.

There's more power in the words
left unsaid. Their last conversation
was a tedious waltz around
the dead body of lust,

his memory unshaken, her pleading eyes
overlapping the fish-eyed naivety,
her pale flesh the thin barrier
between forgiveness and rape.

No. The empty bottles robbed her
of this word he chose to speak for her.

He would have killed them,
preventing wolves from removing
the jewelry from a corpse.

In the light of day
he fools himself into believing
it's the alcohol that does it,
not that all men have sharks in their skin
waiting for paper cuts
from the lips of the moon.

Materialism and moving

I often lie about materialism.
I tell myself I am not a victim
of that American cliché,
making a home
from giant gas station drinking cups,
pretending that Tyler Durden
once turned my fist into a revolver.

But when moving,
I don't pile the cluttered mass
of my belongings in the yard
and set it ablaze,
ready to start anew
like some cicada
emerging from the slick, wet ground.

No, I gather my life into boxes,
each object feeling like a tethered
extension of my consciousness,
a verification of my being,
proof I am or I was here, alive,
scratching my head into dust.

My wife stops and reads old love letters
from the boy who deflowered her.
She puts my birthday cards
into a different box.
Later, when shopping for furniture,
we wear each other down:
she prefers the circles,
while I prefer the squares.

Chalk outlines of a future self

I will leave the water running while I brush my teeth,
because it soothes me. Being wasteful can be soothing.
I wonder if every bad habit can be traced to a moment
when the mind was a doorway an elephant wanted through,
to an older self wanting to shrug off his shell
before his skin was hard enough for sun.

I remember that white room with the bunk beds
and the lanky step-cousin with her long brown hair
and glasses, how she offered to teach me to French kiss,
some kind of euphoric burning in my chest
that felt like a moon being born from lungs,
the alternating textures of rough and smooth tongue
on my own, the sweet taste of her hot breath.
 A secret to carry like a moth in my heart.

Two years later, standing in a barn loft,
yellow beams of light glinting between the dark gray boards,
my pants down around my ankles as she said, "Now, stick it in."
Different kids, playing with adult desires like toddlers
slobbering on alphabet blocks. Prepubescent, it was impossible,
yet my penis burned for days where it had touched her.
Another memory, a chalk outline of my future self.

Watching the pink forms of writhing limbs between locked fingers,
became sneaking into an older cousin's magazine stash,
the one I carried home and hid under my mattress
torched in the trash barrel to unclench God's fist,
became staying up all night recording sex scenes from Cinemax,
became sneaking pornography home from the video store,

my grandmother's handwritten note that she had found them.
These layers of dust make the mind a musty attic of shame and lust,
a place where a mother's voice saying, "Turn off the faucet,"
can be the same as one saying, "Close your eyes. Don't look."

It's selfish to demand honesty

the butterflies will never love you,
they will suffocate without knowing
their beauty conjured a fluttering
that demanded to be owned,
their still deaths becoming honesty incarnate.

she wouldn't love you
unless you put her in a jar,
when you looked through her phone
there were used condoms filled with wine,
a clumsy confessional that ripped curtains
like screams from a ventricle.

and now we are Pyramus and Thisbe,
each in a jar side by side,
mouthing the words through the glass,
tapping wedding rings in Morse code
just to feel each other's vibration,
while watching each other die.

ACKNOWLEDGEMENTS

Some of these poems have previously appeared in online or print publications, and I give my thanks to the editors that took chances on my work.

"Job interview," appeared in *Scissors and Spackle*.
"Narcissism born," appeared in *ExFic*.
"Adult Film Actress," appeared in *Wild Goose Poetry Review*.
"Ken and Barbie," appeared in *Wilderness House Literary Review*.
"My new bed," appeared in *Ayris*.
"Admissions," and "Habits," both appeared in the Skinning Honesty Anthology from *Nostrovia*.
"Almost date raped," appeared in *Unlikely Stories*.
"Chalk outlines of a future self," appeared at *Vending Machine Press*.

ABOUT THE AUTHOR

Jay Sizemore doesn't win awards. He writes poems and stories and scribbles his name a lot onto electronic pads for material possessions. He listens to Ryan Adams and drinks Four Roses. You can find his work online in places if you go looking, including his chapbook Father Figures, still available on Amazon. His wife puts up with his shit in Nashville, TN. Find him at http://www.jaysizemore.com.